WHAT'S GOING ON IN WW2?

Paul Mason

D0486974

Published 2011
First published in hardback 2010 by
A&C Black Publishers Ltd.
36 Soho Square, London, W1D 3QY

www.acblack.com

ISBN 978-1-4081-2680-6

Series consultant: Gill Matthews

Text copyright © 2010 Paul Mason

Some of the quotes in this book are fictional and are designed to illustrate what it might have been like to experience the events recorded.

The right of Paul Mason to be identified as the author of this work has been asserted by him in accordance with the Copyrights, Designs and Patents Act 1988.

A CIP catalogue for this book is available from the British Library.

Every effort has been made to trace copyright holders and to obtain their permission for use of copyright material. The author and publishers would be pleased to rectify any error or omission in future editions.

This book is produced using paper that is made from wood grown in managed, sustainable forests. It is natural, renewable and recyclable. The logging and manufacturing processes conform to the environmental regulations of the country of origin.

Produced for A&C Black by Calcium. www.calciumcreative.co.uk

Printed and bound in China by C&C Offset Printing Co.

All the internet addresses given in this book were correct at the time of going to press. The author and publishers regret any inconvenience caused if addresses have changed or sites have ceased to exist, but can accept no responsibility for any such changes.

Acknowledgements

The publishers would like to thank the following for their kind permission to reproduce their photographs:

Cover: Shutterstock. **Pages:** Corbis: Bettmann 17; Fotolia: Alexey Shadrin 13; Getty Images: William Vandivert/Life Magazine/Time & Life Pictures 24; Library of Congress: 5; National Archives and Records Admini[stration 4, 8, 10, 16, 19, 20, 22, 23] ... [US] Navy/Conseil Régional de Basse-Normandie ... [...]a Press 18, 26; Shutterstock: Timothy R. Nicho[...] ...[...]ate (CPHOM) Robert F. Sargent, U.S. Coast G[uard] ... [...]edia Commons: 6r, 9, 12, 15b, 29r, National Arc[hives and Records Admini...] Army Air Force 23b.

CONTENTS

POLAND INVADED!

Yesterday, Polish men, women, and children hid in terror as German tanks rolled past their doors. "The ground shook as the tanks went by," said one woman. "We hid in our **cellar** for 14 hours, with nothing to eat."

German soldiers prepare to throw a grenade at Polish forces

Polish forces retreat

Poland's army is **retreating** from the border with Germany. "We are falling back to the east," reported a grim-faced Polish officer, "to places where we will be able to destroy their tanks. Then the Germans will have a hard fight on their hands. But we need help from other countries."

Bütgenbach

Lunebach

The German leader, Adolf Hitler, is responsible for the attacks on Poland.

BACKGROUND TO THE ATTACK

The attack has happened because the German leader, Adolf Hitler, claims that parts of western Poland belong to Germany. Many German speakers live in the area. Hitler says they want to be part of Germany, not Poland.

Help from abroad?

Polish leaders hope for help from Great Britain and France. The three countries are **Allies**. These countries have joined forces to fight Germany.

The Allies have said Germany must not invade Poland, but it is not clear what else they can do to help. The whole of Germany lies between them and Poland.

Burg-Reuland Habscheid

ouvy

JEWS TO BE SENT EAST

There was widespread disbelief and horror among German Jews yesterday, as the **Nazi** government announced that Jews must pack up and leave the country.

JEWS FORBIDDEN

Polish Jews were the first to be rounded up by Nazis. Now the German Jews have met the same fate.

Horrified reactions

"My family has lived here for hundreds of years," said one Jewish shopkeeper, who did not want to be named. "I fought for Germany in the First World War. Why must I leave? This makes no sense."

Trains to the East

The government is arranging trains to take Jewish families east. They are to live in **ghettos** – places where only Jews can live. Government forces will begin to round up Jewish families in the next few days.

NAZI GERMANY AND THE JEWS

The Nazis have taken many steps against the Jews since Hitler became leader in 1933:

- In 1933, Jews were banned from working as teachers, judges, doctors, and lawyers.

- From 1935, Jews were no longer allowed to be German **citizens.**

- From 1935, Jews were not allowed to marry Germans.

- On 9 November 1938, Nazi supporters spent the night smashing up Jewish businesses and **synagogues.**

The burned-out shell of a Jewish synagogue

Burg-Reuland · Habscheid · ouvy

PARIS FALLS!

15.06.1940

The German **conquest** of Europe continues. Last night news reached us that German forces have captured Paris. France now seems sure to surrender.

Hitler in front
of Paris's famous
Eiffel Tower

Allied forces scattered

Germany's fast attack left the Allied forces scattered. Over a million French soldiers were taken prisoner. The ones left behind changed out of their uniforms and slowly made their way home. "It was chaos, utter chaos," one Frenchman told me. "The Germans just kept coming. It was completely hopeless."

Paris waits

In the French capital, people do not know what to expect. The markets are empty, and the streets are quiet – except for the sound of German patrol tanks driving by.

Evacuation at Dunkirk

Some Allied soldiers did escape from France. Filthy and exhausted, they have been brought across the Channel. "The boys fought their way out," reported Sergeant Major Harris of the Guards Regiment. "And they've lived to fight another day. I'm very proud."

Exhuasted soldiers during the battle for France

AN EXCURSION TO HELL

All kinds of boat - battleships, yachts, and lifeboats - brought the troops to England.

"The little holiday steamers made an excursion to hell, and came back glorious,"

said the writer J. B. Priestley, describing the **evacuation** of Dunkirk. *

*From a radio broadcast on 5 June.

Gouvy

Burg-Reuland

Habscheid

BLITZ ON LONDON!

07.11.1940

Germany's bombing of **civilian** Londoners continued last night. Several streets in the East End were flattened. Survivors are still being pulled from the **rubble**.

Smoke drifts in front of the dome of St Paul's Cathedral, London

Early alerts

Shivering on the rooftops in the cold November air, the firewatchers knew the German bombers were coming. First the drone of their engines was heard, and then flashes of exploding bombs were seen in the East End. Another night of the Blitz on London had begun.

Firefighters joined by soldiers

As parts of the city burned, neighbourhood firefighters leapt into action. Without their bravery, a church hall in Greenwich where hundreds of people were sheltering would have burned down.

The firefighters were helped by soldiers at home on **leave**. "I come home for a weekend's rest!" said one **Tommy** with a soot-blackened face, "But you've got to fight Hitler wherever you can, haven't you?"

Londoners still go to work. The bombing has not dampened their spirits.

Spirits remain high

The bombing has not broken people's spirits. "Hitler can eat his hat for all I care," said Gladys Knight, standing in front of her bombed-out house. "Londoners will never give in."

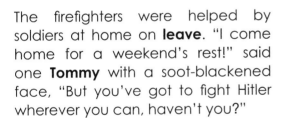

WORDS FROM KING GEORGE VI

"We have now had a personal experience of German barbarity, which only strengthens the **resolution** of all of us to fight through to final victory."

Gouvy Burg-Reuland Habscheid

LENINGRAD UNDER SIEGE!

09.09.1941

The German Army yesterday surrounded the great Soviet city of Leningrad. Leningrad's heroic defenders are readying themselves for a long **siege**.

A Soviet fighter waits to take a shot at the enemy

Germans dig in

Germany's original plan to capture and destroy Leningrad has failed. Now, the Germans will try to starve the city into defeat. To the south, the German Army is preventing supplies getting through. In the north, Germany's Finnish **lapdogs** are doing the same.

Supplies running short

Leningrad's defenders are running low on food. Warehouses full of supplies have been bombed and destroyed by the Germans. There may only be enough left to feed people for four weeks. But the defence will not end – Leningrad's **munitions** factories will make sure that the city does not run out of guns or bullets.

Surviving winter

The freezing weather will make survival harder for Leningrad's people. But Russians are used to snow – and when Lake Ladoga freezes over, supplies will be able to reach the city across the ice.

SHOE SOUP

Civilians in Leningrad are already finding food hard to come by. But Russian resourcefulness knows no boundaries! The people have discovered that boiling up leather shoes for days makes a thin soup.

"It may not be very nice - but it beats starving to death," said Yelena Golunskaya as she stood by her stove.

People wait for Lake Ladoga to freeze...

Burg-Reuland   Habscheid

PEARL HARBOR ATTACKED!

08.12.1941

Destroyed battleships smoulder next to docks, or lie at the bottom of the ocean. Bodies of servicemen rest in their coffins. Yesterday, the horror of war came to American shores.

Smoke pours from destroyed battleships

Surprise attack

Japan's attack on the US navy base at Pearl Harbor took everyone by surprise. "At first we had no idea what was happening," one sailor reported. "The sky was suddenly full of planes. But when the bombs started to fall, we realized we were under attack."

The full extent of the damage is not yet clear. Reports suggest that eight battleships, three cruisers, and three destroyers have been damaged or wrecked. 2,402 people have been killed, and 1,282 wounded.

14

The ships at Pearl Harbor were simply sitting ducks.

PRESIDENT DECLARES WAR

President Roosevelt has declared war on Japan. He announced that: "No matter how long it may take us...the American people in their righteous might will win through to absolute victory."

The **mobilization** of American forces is expected to begin straight away. Meanwhile, anti-aircraft guns are being set up on the beaches and hills of California in case of Japanese attacks.

Islanders terrified

On Hawaii, people are scared. Stories are being told of a Japanese invasion fleet nearing the islands. As far as is known, this is not true. But as one Hawaiian homeowner said: "They didn't think the Japanese aircraft were sneaking up to attack us, either."

Japanese fighter planes line up to begin the attack

Gouvy Burg-Reuland Habscheid

Troisvierges

JAPANESE TAKE MANILA

02.01.1942

The American flag no longer flies over Manila. The Japanese yesterday captured the city. However, the determined US and Philippines forces fight on.

US soldiers surrender to the Japanese in Manila

Bodies all over

It has taken Japan's troops almost a month to reach Manila. "We made them pay in blood for every inch," one of the **Filipino** fighters told your reporter. "Our people will never stop fighting the invaders."

Resistance continues

Filipino **resistance fighters** are still attacking the Japanese from their bases in the mountains. Meanwhile, US forces are withdrawing to the Bataan **Peninsula**. The battle for Bataan is expected to be the fiercest of the war so far.

DARWIN BOMBED!

Australians ran for their lives yesterday as Japanese bombs fell on the city of Darwin. The bombing has killed hundreds of people and destroyed many buildings.

These Australian servicemen discovered a Japanese fighter plane that crashed during the bombing.

Australia's Pearl Harbor

Like Pearl Harbor, the Japanese attack took Darwin by surprise. "One minute everything was like normal. The next, we were running for cover. The bombs were falling like fleas off a **dingo**," said Ed MacMahon, of MacMahon's Hardware.

Damage to ships, loss of life

Eight ships have been sunk in the harbour, and many Allied aircraft destroyed. Worse, over 200 people, including many civilians, have been killed. "No Aussie minds a fair fight," said MacMahon, "but this wasn't a fair fight."

VICTORY AT STALINGRAD

03.02.1943

Weak with hunger, hollow-cheeked, and surrounded by ruined buildings, the people of Stalingrad nonetheless last night threw a party. Why? The Battle of Stalingrad is finally over.

A Soviet soldier attacks a German position

From the city

"I always knew we would win," said Oleg Karpov, who has been defending Stalingrad since July 1942. "Still, it'll be good to be able to walk down the street without worrying about German **snipers**. And I'm looking forward to having more to eat – it's as hard to find food here as it was in Leningrad!"

A turning point?

Is victory at Stalingrad a turning point in the war? One solider certainly thought so. Looking around at the ruined city, he made a grim promise: "In the end, Berlin will look worse."

Defeated German soldiers
march through Stalingrad

STALINGRAD: THE COST

Both sides have paid a
high price in the Battle
of Stalingrad. In total,
roughly two million people
have died in the fighting.

- Almost the whole
  city is now rubble.
  Few buildings are
  still standing.

- At times during the
  battle, the Germans
  controlled 90 per cent
  of the city, and the
  Russians held only the
  west bank of the Volga River.

- In November 1942, as the weather became
  cold, the Russians attacked. They surrounded
  the German 6th Army.

- Most Germans surrendered in February 1943.
  A few carried on fighting. They hid in
  cellars and **sewers**. By March, all had
  been killed or captured.

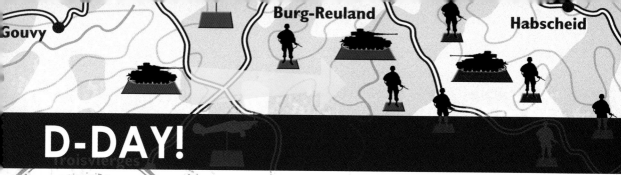

Gouvy Burg-Reuland Habscheid

D-DAY!

Aboard our landing craft, men crossed themselves, clutched lucky charms, or simply stared ahead. Then, suddenly, the boat lurched to a stop. The ramp at the front dropped, and the soldiers charged forwards. Their attempt to liberate France began.

Paratroops first in

The first Allied troops in France were British and US paratroopers. They floated down through a sky full of German bullets, just after midnight. Their job was to capture and hold key roads, bridges, and hills. This has stopped German **reinforcements** reaching the landing sites on the coast.

Allied paratroopers rain down in northern France

The view as Allied soldiers wade ashore in Northern France

Beach landings

Just after dawn, the first Allied troops began to land on the beaches of France. British, Canadian, and American soldiers attacked five main landing sites. Despite coming under heavy fire as they waded ashore, the determined troops have successfully pushed the Germans back.

ESTABLISHING A BRIDGEHEAD

Allied soldiers are now battling to establish a **bridgehead** on the French coast. They need a secure area where more troops and supplies can safely be landed. Once this has happened, the Allies will break out of the bridgehead and begin the long fight towards Germany itself.

Trucks and men pour ashore to begin the fight

IWO JIMA CAPTURED

Yesterday, the tiny Pacific island of Iwo Jima was at last captured. Small pockets of resistance remain as the Japanese fight to the death, but US troops now control the island.

High cost of success

Many thousands of US **Marines** have been killed or injured. The cost to the Japanese has been even higher. "They fought to the death," said one Marine. "I don't think any surrendered." Of over 20,000 Japanese soldiers, only 216 were captured alive.

US Marines advance on Iwo Jima

TOKYO BOUND

Bomber pilots on their way to an air raid on Japan

Super-fortresses can now reach Japan

Iwo Jima's airstrips can now be used for bombing raids against Japan's cities. Bombers from Iwo Jima are expected to join the air raids on Tokyo very soon.

Fires smoulder in an area of Tokyo destroyed by bombing

RAIDS ON TOKYO

US bombers have now destroyed a quarter of Tokyo, Japan's capital city. Experts suggest that 100,000 people have died, and 1.5 million have been made **homeless.**

While regretting any loss of civilian lives, we should remember three important points:

- Many civilians have died because of Japanese aggression.

- The raids have destroyed Japan's arms factories — wrecking their ability to fight on in the war.

- Ending the war will mean that the suffering of people in lands controlled by the Japanese will soon be over.

US TROOPS CROSS RHINE

23.03.1945

By now, the news must have reached Hitler's **bunker** in Berlin. Yesterday, General Patton's Third Army crossed the River Rhine, and entered the heartland of Germany.

US troops step ashore after crossing the Rhine

Nazi dream in tatters

Twelve days ago American soldiers entered Germany for the first time. The advance must have come as a further, terrible blow to Hitler. Now the **dictator** who once dreamed of enslaving Europe faces final defeat.

Germans on the run

"The Germans are on the run now," said Corporal E. Robert Spiers of the 99th Infantry Division. "It's a race to see who gets to Berlin first – us, or the Russians."

HORROR IN THE FOREST

13.04.1945

The people clinging to the wire fences are as thin as skeletons. Some cannot even stand up. Here and there, tears run down their cheeks – tears of joy. Freedom has come.

Place of death

This camp in the forest is named Belsen, and it is a Nazi death camp. The prisoners are Jews, **gypsies**, **homosexuals**, and others whom the Nazis despised. They had been sent there to work, and to die. Tens of thousands of people, maybe more, have died here.

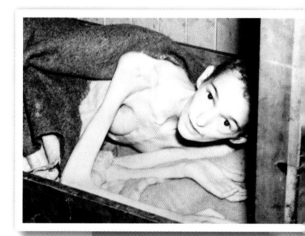

A victim of the Belsen Camp

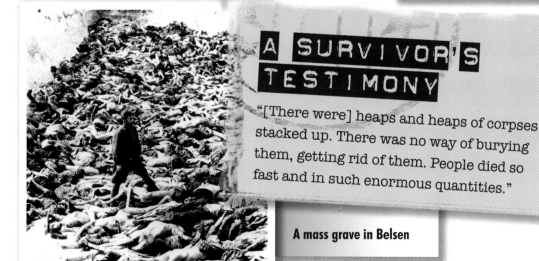

A SURVIVOR'S TESTIMONY

"[There were] heaps and heaps of corpses stacked up. There was no way of burying them, getting rid of them. People died so fast and in such enormous quantities."

A mass grave in Belsen

25

BERLIN TAKEN!

03.05.1945

After fierce fighting, Berlin has finally surrendered. The city has nearly been destroyed by the ferocious Russian attack.

The Soviet flag is raised above the Reichstag, after its capture by Russian troops

A city in ruins

Few of Berlin's buildings are still standing. Everywhere there are piles of bricks; the ruins of houses and offices. People live mostly in cellars, the only rooms that are still intact.

Cleaning up Berlin

The smell of death is everywhere. Groups of civilians have been put to work hunting for bodies in the rubble. Hungry children dart about, looking for food. The Russian Army has started handing out food packages to the starving people.

WORLD REJOICES AS HITLER DIES, BERLIN FALLS

Unable to bear the defeat of his armies, Hitler and his wife Eva killed themselves on 30 April 1945. Berlin surrendered soon afterwards.

"On the walls of Berlin's houses we saw appeals, hurriedly scrawled in white paint: 'We shall stop the Red hordes at the walls of our Berlin.' Just try and stop them!"

– *A Russian war correspondent describes the Soviet Army's entry into Berlin.*

"Hitler? He got what he deserved, I'd say. It's just a shame it was the Russians, not our boys that got there first."

– *Jeb Turner, a worker at the Lockheed aircraft factory in California, USA.*

"It won't make up for what happened in the Blitz, but I'm glad that man's dead."

– *Beryl Tewkes, queuing outside a butcher's shop in Isleworth, London.*

Allied soldiers advance through Berlin

NAGASAKI HIT BY A-BOMB

10.08.1945

On August 6, the Japanese city of Hiroshima was destroyed by an atomic bomb. Yesterday, another atomic bomb was dropped on the city of Nagasaki, reducing it to rubble.

President approves bombings

Both of the devastating A-bomb attacks on Japan were approved by President Truman. He hopes that the terrible power of the bombs will bring the war to a quick end. So far, though, there has been no response from any of Japan's leaders.

Will Japan surrender?

The Allies demanded a Japanese surrender on 26 July. They said that non-surrender would result in, "the utter devastation of the Japanese homeland." Japan's leaders must now believe that this is true.

A mushroom cloud rises into the sky after the atomic explosion

JAPAN SURRENDERS

Today, on the decks of the aircraft carrier USS Missouri, Japan formally surrendered. The surrender ended the war that has engulfed the world since 1939.

02.09.1945

US officers accept Japan's surrender

Hirohito admits defeat

On 15 August, Japan's Emperor Hirohito told his people that Japan would surrender. To do otherwise, he said, would mean the Japanese people would be wiped out.

Cost of conflict

How many people have died in the war? As many as 60 million – two-thirds of them civilians. The lives of tens of millions more have been ruined. We can all agree with the shouts of the unnamed **GI** in Times Square. "Thank God it's over!"

Emperor Hirohito, Japan's head of state

GLOSSARY

Allies group of countries who acted together during World War II, led by Great Britain, the USA, and Russia

bridgehead secure area where troops and supplies can land

bunker underground stronghold

cellar underground storage room

citizens people who are allowed to live in a country all their life

civilian person who is not part of the military forces

conquest to take control of a place and the people that live there

dictator person who rules people with force and does not listen to their views

dingo kind of wild dog found in Australia

evacuation moving away from a place of danger

Filipino person from the Philippines

ghettos areas of cities where people the Germans persecuted were forced to live

GI nickname for American soldiers (short for either Government Issue or General Infantry)

gypsies people who travel from place to place

homeless people without a permanent place to live

homosexuals people who are attracted to the same sex

lapdogs people who obey orders without question

leave holiday from military service

marines soldiers in the navy

mobilization the preparation of armed forces for war

munitions military supplies, including weapons

Nazi member of the National Socialist German Workers' Party that ruled Germany from 1933 to 1945.

peninsula area of land that sticks out into the sea or a lake

reinforcements extra soldiers

resistance fighters people who fight against an invader, but are not part of the official armed forces

resolution determination to do something

retreating withdrawing or moving back from someone or something

rubble pieces of brick left behind when a building is smashed to bits

sewers channels through which waste water can flow

siege situation in which people are trapped inside a city because they are being attacked by an enemy

snipers soldiers who lie hidden waiting to shoot at enemies

synagogues places where Jewish people go to worship

Tommy nickname for English soldiers

FURTHER INFORMATION

Websites

Find out more about World War II at the
Imperial War Museum:
www.iwm.org.uk

Discover more about what life was like in World War II at:
www.bbc.co.uk/schools/primaryhistory/world_war2

Books

The Second World War by Paul Dowswell. Usborne (2005).

World War II by Reg Grant. Dorling Kindersley (2008).

Hiding Edith by Kathy Kacer. A&C Black (2009).

Movies and DVDs

Tora! Tora! Tora! (1970)
This shows the events leading up to the Japanese
attack on Pearl Harbor in December 1941.

The Sands of Iwo Jima (1948)
John Wayne stars in the tale of the fierce battle to take
the tiny island of Iwo Jima from the Japanese.

INDEX